BE
UNSTOPPABLE

The Art of Never Giving Up

BE UNSTOPPABLE

The Art of Never Giving Up

BETHANY HAMILTON

Photography by
AARON LIEBER

ZONDERVAN

For all the people who have helped and supported me
in my surfing career along the way

—BETHANY

ZONDERVAN

Be Unstoppable

Copyright © 2018 by Surfs Like A Girl, LLC

This title is also available as a Zondervan ebook.

Requests for information should be addressed to:
Zondervan, 3900 Sparks Dr. SE, Grand Rapids, Michigan 49546

ISBN 978-0-310-76485-4

Photos by Aaron Lieber unless otherwise noted.
Photos: page 32 © Mike Curley; pages 66, 70 © Elliot Lebo; pages 74, 76, 84 © Mike Nulty;
        pages 82, 104, 124 © Tim McKenna; page 96 © Tom Servais;
        pages 110, 114, 116, 118 © Agustin Muñoz

Interior design: Ron Huizinga

Printed in China

18 19 20 21 /LPC/ 22 21 20 19 18 17 16 15 14 13 12 11 10 9 8 7 6 5 4 3 2 1

It's been a joy just to be part of Bethany's journey and see what she's been able to accomplish. I always knew what she was capable of, but the level she's at now is pretty incredible. She definitely gives it her best, and she surprises a lot of people.

—TOM HAMILTON,
Bethany's first surfing coach (and dad)

I started working with Bethany because I saw that she was one of the best female surfers in the world, but no one had properly captured it. Over the four years of filming *Unstoppable*, we faced a lot of uncertainty and challenges. But I realized early on that I didn't need all the answers. I just needed to have faith, to be resourceful, to enjoy the process, and to surround Bethany and myself with amazing people who could help make it possible. I hope this book and movie sparks an idea in you—to work hard, to adapt, to enjoy the process and never give up. With hard work, a dream that may seem impossible can eventually become a reality.

—AARON LIEBER,
filmmaker, *Bethany Hamilton: Unstoppable*

ALOHA!

I'm Bethany. I'm known as a professional surfer, but I'm also a wife, mom, health enthusiast, motivational speaker, Christian, and more. I'm stoked to be sharing this book with you! It's full of photos and messages I hope will inspire you to follow your dreams.

I've had a massive passion for surfing and the ocean ever since I was a young girl growing up in Hawaii. In the water, I felt invincible, so at eight years old I set my sights on becoming the best surfer I could be.

But I've found life doesn't always go the way we plan. In 2003, while surfing, a fateful encounter with a shark resulted in the loss of my left arm. I felt as though my hopes had been stripped away, my future left unknown. At times, I struggled with depression, insecurity, and fear, but my faith in God was greater than my hardships. Having hope in God's promise strengthened me to be brave. Through my personal

drive and the support of my family, I recommitted to my passion. Even with one arm and some doubt, I was determined to get in the ocean again and surf.

I'm happy to say I achieved my dream. I'm a professional surfer with a one-of-a-kind career path. The route I envisioned at eight years old shifted dramatically over time, but I wouldn't change a thing. For the last four years, I have partnered with the talented film director Aaron Lieber to create the exciting documentary *Bethany Hamilton: Unstoppable*. This film highlights the awesome journey of my life, and my pursuit to tackle the most challenging surf conditions around the world and become the best surfer I can be. Through making the film, we captured the photos you'll see in this book.

This was a dream journey for me—traveling to surf some of the best waves in the world, working

hard toward my personal surfing goals of riding some of the biggest and most challenging waves. But it wasn't always easy. I had some major wipeouts and unexpected life changes along the way.

It can be hard to hold on to your dreams. I know many of you face some of the same things that I've dealt with—fears, insecurities, failures, and pressures—and I want to encourage you to follow your passion just as fiercely as I've followed mine. My hope is that this book and the film will inspire you to pursue your heart's desire and stick with it even through tough times. Remember, the best things in life don't come easy, so persevere, overcome, and **BE UNSTOPPABLE!**

I'm so thankful to have grown up in Hawaii, the birthplace of surfing. Surfing here has made me the surfer I am in a lot of ways, especially with access to bigger, more powerful waves, and having a family of chargers to push my own determination to charge! I was challenged at an early age to overcome a fear of big waves. And I continued to overcome that as I grew up.

So many incredible surfers are from these islands. As my friend and fellow Hawaii surfer Coco Ho has said, "We were ahead of the game because of each other collectively." It is so true. Talent and inspiration constantly surrounded me every time I paddled out to surf.

From beach breaks to powerful point breaks and everything in between, Hawaii is a breeding ground for well-rounded surfers. And I love this simple lifestyle: all you need is a bikini and surfboard to have a great adventure.

The challenge of my life has always been to exceed my own expectations and push my limits. What inspires me is simple: being the best I can be in whatever I'm doing.

Even though I'm an experienced surfer and I feel confident in my ability, it took a long time and a lot of support to get here. I thrive off coaching—it gives me that extra edge. I love advice on how to get better and improve myself.

Adapting takes time and persistence.
There are days of struggle, but that doesn't stop me
from learning and practicing.

★

I've had to deal with some big fears: One, my arm's gone, so how am I going to face my future? And two, sharks will always be in the ocean. But I believe we can do amazing things when we focus on our abilities rather than our fears.

I want to be more than just a
surfer. I want to honor God
with my life.

Anyone can chase their passions, goals, and dreams—and rock their sport. I totally believe it's possible. You can achieve more than you know. Work hard, have fun, and love much!

True love means faithfulness, friendship, romance, kindness, security, selflessness, and sharing life together. Be patient; true love is well worth waiting for.

Indonesia is known in the surfing world for its amazing surf breaks. Imagine thousands of islands and thousands of really good waves. Throughout my surfing career, I've spent more time surfing Indo than any other foreign country. It keeps drawing me back.

We took two trips to Indo for the film, and on our second trip we decided to venture over to an outer island to surf one of my favorite waves in the world, Macaronis. The journey to get there was crazy. After the overseas flights, we had to take two in-country flights and an overnight ferry ride on a rusty boat with a lot of local passengers, millions of bananas in tow, and cockroaches crawling all over us!

When we got to Macaronis, the waves were perfect, barreling lefts. It was like your favorite ride at the fair; you keep going on it again and again. I surfed for eight hours straight the first day without leaving the water. Friends brought snacks and drinks out to me. I surfed my brains out, and later my body was feeling it. Even so, the next day, I surfed six more hours!

NDONESIA

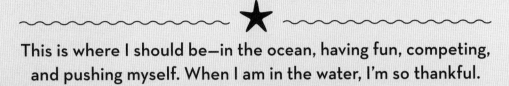

This is where I should be—in the ocean, having fun, competing, and pushing myself. When I am in the water, I'm so thankful.

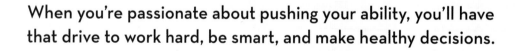

When you're passionate about pushing your ability, you'll have that drive to work hard, be smart, and make healthy decisions.

Do the best you can
with what you've been given.

BALI

When I headed down to Bali, I had recently finished a focused coaching session with Shane Beschen to work on my aerials, so I was hoping to put some of that coaching to practice in the ocean. In one session, where the waves were really fun and the lineup of surfers was not too crowded, I was catching a ton of waves. While paddling back out from a ride, I saw a great wave coming right for me. I quickly turned around and caught it. On that wave, I pulled off one of the best maneuvers of my life—an air reverse—without putting too much thought into it. It felt incredibly amazing! That moment was a catalyst to push my above-the-lip (aerial) surfing.

If you really want something,
you'll go after it.

One of my coaches really got me thinking when he said that nerves, pressure, and anxiety really don't exist. They're only created by the thoughts you put in your head.

★

Not all roses are red. Not all roses are perfect.
But all roses have something beautiful about them!
As we go through life, we may not be perfect, but there is
something gorgeous about each of us.

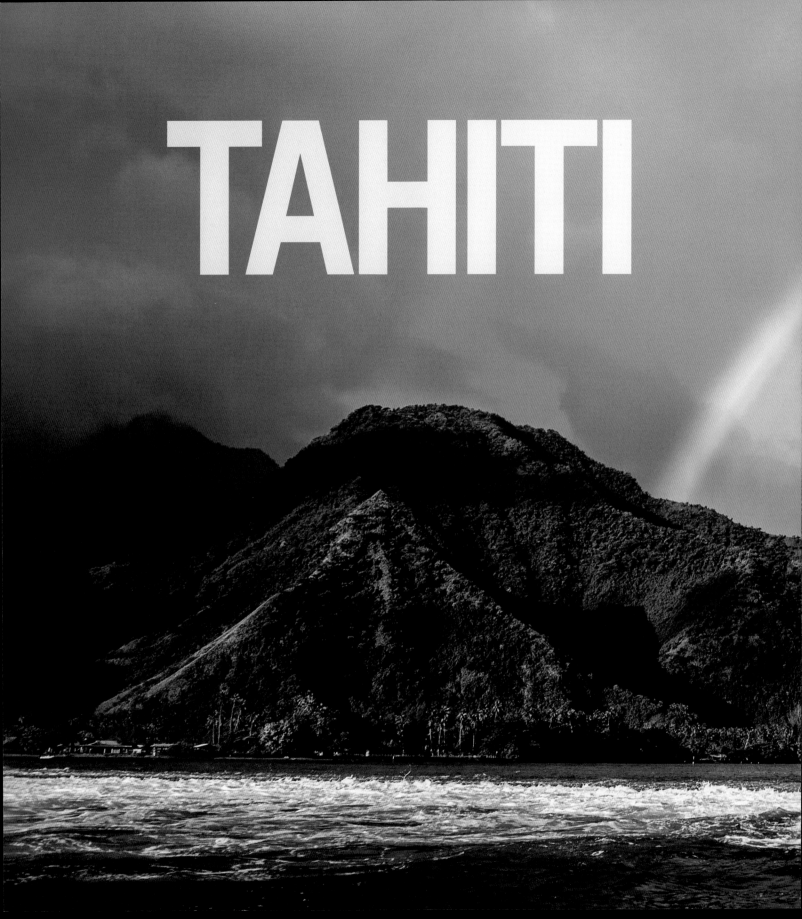

TAHITI

Tahiti is one of the most majestic places in the world. I'm attracted to it because it reminds me of home, Hawaii, but it's like going back in time. The wave named Teahupo'o is known for its power and beauty; it's one of the most breathtaking waves and the ultimate ride for a surfer. However, things were not coming together on this trip. For five of the six days we were there, the waves were so bad that I didn't get to surf once. Plus, I was having headaches and felt tired and emotional; I didn't know why. Even though I rode a few fun waves on the one day I did surf, we didn't accomplish the overall purpose of our trip, leaving us disappointed. That's the nature of the ocean; it's unpredictable.

Surfing has so many ups and downs. I can have an amazing performance in one session and then fall apart in the next— and I'm halfway across the world, far from the comforts of home. It's important to be aware of the challenges you're facing and how they affect you emotionally; know that awesomeness can still come out of hard work.

Often, through difficult times, we have the opportunity to grow, mature, and learn our strengths. Or, those challenges may show weaknesses that we can work on and overcome. So when I don't achieve a goal, I still focus on why I'm doing what I'm doing each day. Knowing why and being passionate naturally keep me motivated.

"My flesh and my heart may fail, but God is the strength of my heart and my portion forever."

—Psalm 73:26

UNEXPECTED
GIFTS

A month or so after our trip to Tahiti, I realized I was pregnant. I felt like my life turned upside down. Our plans for the film and my career seemed uncertain. We had planned to release *Unstoppable* that coming summer, but we still had more trips I needed to complete. With a baby growing inside me, how long would I be able to surf? How would the changes in my body affect my performance and ability to get the job done? Did I still want to pursue a surfing career, or should I focus solely on being a mom? I was unsure of so much!

Once Adam and my fears faded, we were excited about becoming parents. Surfing had always been one of the most important things in my life, until my family began to grow. With the support of my husband and our team, we decided to continue and keep sight of my surfing goals.

I continued surfing until it was too uncomfortable—around seven months pregnant. One cool thing was that surfing pregnant actually improved my style. Because of the changes in my body, I had to do slower, more drawn-out turns, which smoothed out my surfing overall. But the best thing was finally meeting our son, Tobias, who is one of our greatest joys.

My identity is first in who
God has made me. That can't
be stripped away.

I like the challenge of staying strong and fit.
And I love when I can feel that strength carry over into my
surfing. It's such a rewarding feeling.

No matter what comes
my way, God is going
to sustain me.

★

The ocean is my happy place.
Even if I'm frustrated with my
surfing or having a bad day,
I can get in the water and
feel like I had my ocean time.
It's been my love, a place of
healing and reflection, and
the place where I can
just be me.

LOWER TRESTLES
CALIFORNI

A

I loved re-setting my goals after having a baby. I was so honored when I learned I was being given the wild card for the World Surfing League Swatch Women's Pro in 2015. I found out about a month and a half after Tobias was born, and I thought, *Oh my gosh, my abs are separated and I haven't surfed in over three months. I've got my work cut out for me.* My task felt difficult, and getting back in shape in time for the event was going to take a lot of discipline. It felt amazing to work hard to regain my fitness and dust the cobwebs off my surfboard. By the time I got to the contest, I was ready and physically back to normal.

Goals are so valuable. When you have something to reach toward—a goal of any kind, big or small—it feels amazing to see the outcome of each step along the way.

As enthusiastic as I am about staying healthy and strong, it is important to rest when I need to and not overdo it. Our bodies work hard, and we need to care for them.

I've always wanted to push my big wave surfing and take on the infamous Pe'ahi "Jaws" at its best. Six months after I had a baby, the conditions aligned and I was on a plane to Maui to do just that. To surf big waves, I spend so much time thinking on it, hoping for it, training, prepping, planning, and then going for it. My first session at Jaws was a tow-in session, where a jet ski whipped me into the biggest waves of my life. I was on cloud nine!

The next week, I paddled into Jaws; it was hands down the scariest surf of my life. Adrenaline was surging through my body the entire day. I just had to put my head down and go.

It's terrifying and exciting, and like one of the best big wave surfers, Greg Long, says about Jaws: "There's nothing else I've ever seen or experienced that even comes close to that wave, and that's what draws us all there year after year, swell after swell."

JAWS
MAUI

You can't halfheartedly
go for your dreams.
You just have to go.

When I approach a big wave,
I have to see the wave far in
advance and start paddling
early. With Jaws, part of
me thought, *It will be hard,
but it's doable.* It's such an
accomplishment to overcome
the doubts we may have in
our abilities.

I'd heard people say how hard it would be to paddle into the wave at Jaws with one arm. That comment stuck in my brain, so I wanted to overcome it. I didn't want that to be my reason for not trying.

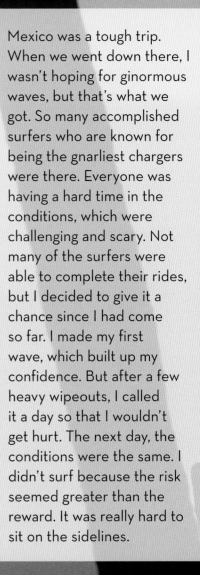

Mexico was a tough trip. When we went down there, I wasn't hoping for ginormous waves, but that's what we got. So many accomplished surfers who are known for being the gnarliest chargers were there. Everyone was having a hard time in the conditions, which were challenging and scary. Not many of the surfers were able to complete their rides, but I decided to give it a chance since I had come so far. I made my first wave, which built up my confidence. But after a few heavy wipeouts, I called it a day so that I wouldn't get hurt. The next day, the conditions were the same. I didn't surf because the risk seemed greater than the reward. It was really hard to sit on the sidelines.

Courage doesn't mean you
don't get afraid. Courage
means you don't let fear stop
you from trying.

Wipeouts are inevitable. The immediate reaction while underwater is to fight your way out of it. But struggling and fighting will make you lose oxygen faster. So even when it's a small wipeout, I practice immediately relaxing. Then when the big wipeouts happen, it is more natural to stay calm.

Sometimes, there are things in life that are not understandable. As a Christian, in whatever I go through, this verse reminds me that God is in control: "Trust in the Lord with all your heart, and do not lean on your own understanding. In all your ways acknowledge him, and he will make straight your paths." (Proverbs 3:5–6)

Everyone has their setbacks. But often what we focus on—the positive or the negative—directs our outcome. If you think you can overcome it, you will. If you think you can't, you won't.

Wiping out is part of life.
But you have the choice to
paddle back out.

Many of us would probably
do a lot more with our lives
if we just believed we could.
You might even exceed your
expectations.

The Maldives are on the opposite side of the world from Hawaii, so it's one of the farthest places I traveled to. We went there for a specific wave called Pasta Point, and a surf coach came with me so I could focus on my aerial surfing. My friend, Lakey Peterson, came along too. Lakey is great at doing airs and has a strong backside approach. Having a surf buddy motivated me to surf my best.

With a sport like surfing that depends on the weather and the swells, sometimes there will be big disappointments and other times great successes. The wave conditions on this trip were challenging to surf, let alone ideal to work on my airs. So we had a lot of time to play games, drink coffee, and work out.

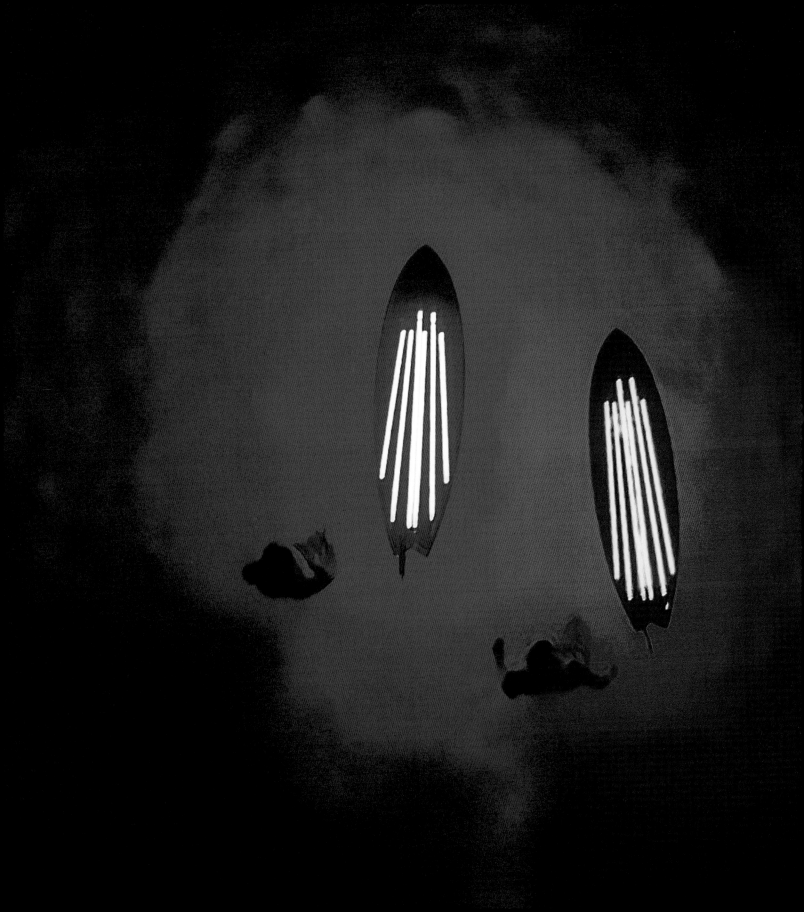

I've definitely faced times
when I've felt down. It's
important to have community
so that when those times
come, you have people you
can talk to. My friends and
family encouraged me to
keep my eyes on Christ.
My mom would pray and
read the Bible with me. I
found encouragement in
God's Word.

Night surfing is so
exhilarating. You really gotta
rely on your natural senses
and ignore your fears.

The mind is so powerful. If I'm thinking about something negative, I'll tend to fall more. It's like I lose the strength in my body. But if I'm thinking positive, and have a good attitude, I'm likely to surf a lot better. Be mindful of your thoughts and attitudes when working toward your goals.

All of us go through situations that are hard to face, but adversity really can make us stronger. So, find what gives you strength to push past the hardest of hard times.

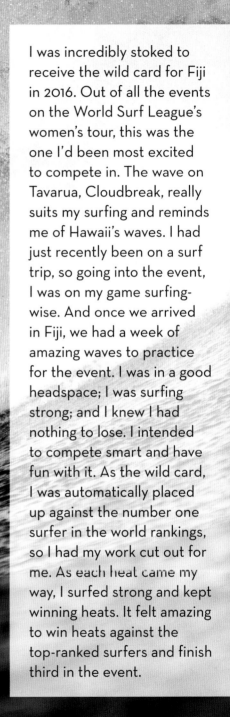

I was incredibly stoked to receive the wild card for Fiji in 2016. Out of all the events on the World Surf League's women's tour, this was the one I'd been most excited to compete in. The wave on Tavarua, Cloudbreak, really suits my surfing and reminds me of Hawaii's waves. I had just recently been on a surf trip, so going into the event, I was on my game surfing-wise. And once we arrived in Fiji, we had a week of amazing waves to practice for the event. I was in a good headspace; I was surfing strong; and I knew I had nothing to lose. I intended to compete smart and have fun with it. As the wild card, I was automatically placed up against the number one surfer in the world rankings, so I had my work cut out for me. As each heat came my way, I surfed strong and kept winning heats. It felt amazing to win heats against the top-ranked surfers and finish third in the event.

When it comes to achieving dreams and goals, there are so many key ingredients: passion, drive, dedication, commitment, and support from people around you.

What better life than to be
able to love and support
other people.

I'm not going to let the fact that I lost an arm change the way I view myself as an athlete. I don't look at it like, "Wow, I did a really good job with one arm." It's just, "Wow, I did a good job on that wave." It's all about perspective.

Focus on being "beautiful you" inside and out.
True beauty in God's eyes is when you "let your adorning be
the hidden person of the heart with the imperishable beauty
of a gentle and quiet spirit, which in God's sight
is very precious." (1 Peter 3:4)

Many people let what others
think of them affect how
they live their lives. I choose
to pursue my passions—faith,
family, and surfing. Those are
the things that matter.

COSTA RI

CA

We went down to Costa Rica so I could prepare for the Fiji Women's Pro and get some solid time in the water. It's rare to find surf spots with minimal to no crowds. I heard about a secret spot that had an amazing left-breaking wave. Taking a trip to a place like this gave me an opportunity to train hard in my surfing. It was also a special family time and Tobias' first trip outside the USA. Since it was safe and quiet there, I got to have fun playing with him on the beach. We played tourist a little bit too and saw alligators.

We can adapt and thrive in
this challenging world, and
we can bring hope to others
in their challenges.

★

I love how the ocean is always changing. Every time I surf, it's different than the time before. No one wave is like another; it's both challenging and refreshing. For me, it's like art, seeing what I can create on each wave.

Surfing with one arm is so
normal to me now that I can't
remember surfing with
two arms.

Through our imperfections,
we can show beauty and
goodness to others, as well as
glorify God through what we
overcome.

Grace is one thing we cannot live without: "For by grace you have been saved through faith. And this is not your own doing; it is the gift of God, not a result of works, so that no one may boast."
(Ephesians 2:8–9)

SURF LIFE

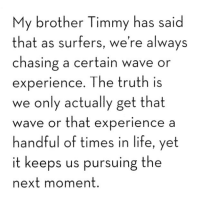

My brother Timmy has said that as surfers, we're always chasing a certain wave or experience. The truth is we only actually get that wave or that experience a handful of times in life, yet it keeps us pursuing the next moment.

After watching the Tahiti swell forecast for two years, looking and waiting for a particular type of swell, the conditions finally looked promising. We were on a plane to Papeete within forty-eight hours. We were hopeful, but unsure it would be all that we hoped it would be.

★

Tahiti turned out to be one
of the highlights in my surfing
career! I was able to surf
huge waves at Teahupo'o and
got some of the best barrels
of my life.

As I pursued my passion for surfing, I realized I didn't need easy; I just needed possible. That's how I approach life: I look for the possibilities and I work hard toward those.

I never could have imagined
my life as it is now. God's
given me this passion to surf,
and he's using it for his glory.

Bethany has an amazing work ethic. She's so driven. I see that on a day-to-day basis—how hard she works, how passionate she is about her life—and it's amazing to me. I find so much purpose in loving and supporting my wife and raising our son. I wouldn't trade my role as husband and father for anything else in the world.

—Adam Dirks, Bethany's husband

ACKNOWLEDGMENTS

Nothing in the world worth doing is going to be easy. But having the right people around you makes all the difference. This book and associated film would not have been possible without a group of amazing individuals.

A huge thank you to my family, who has always supported me in my surfing and helped shape me into the person I am. Especially Becky—throughout writing this book and filming *Unstoppable*, you have been amazing. Thank you for keeping me organized and on task when needed, and for being a wonderful assistant and sister-in-law!

Thank you to my surf coaches over the years, especially Russell Lewis for helping me believe in my abilities in the key moments of my youth. Also a special thank you to Shane Beschen for most recently helping me push my surfing to higher levels. I am grateful to have learned from these amazing individuals: Ben Aipa, Martin Dunn, Ian Cairns, and Craig Hoshide.

Adam, my husband, for your endless support and getting on this adventure to help me reach my dreams and goals. For your love and patience, for being fun, and for a steady shoulder to lean on.

I love you so much!

Aaron Lieber, for your endless efforts and perseverance to make this project a reality. Cheers to some amazing adventures around the world. Thank you for envisioning and pursuing a way to share my story like never seen before!

Our filmmaker Aaron Lieber would also like to acknowledge:

I want to thank Bethany Hamilton for opening her life to me and allowing me to capture her most vulnerable moments and biggest accomplishments.

Adam Dirks—aka Clark Kent and Bethany's husband. He was instrumental in so many different ways. He was always the steady hand for big decisions and the extra energy when we were tired. Adam has this incredible ability to learn and excel in a matter of minutes. Two great stories that exemplify this: I had an idea to create a children's book. A few days later, Adam had written it. Another time I wanted to get a shot of Adam, Bethany, and Tobias packing all their travel gear, and I wanted to be up high looking straight down. Adam made a few calls, found and borrowed a lift tractor, learned how to use it, and lifted me up high to get the shot.

Thanks to Becky Hamilton, Bethany's executive assistant. Her attention to detail, enthusiasm, and support of the film and book was a key ingredient in our success.

And last, but not least, thank you to my family: my mom, Caron; my dad, Bob; and my sister, Ashley. Between the three of them, I have the dream team of support, criticism, and love.

Aaron, Adam, and I are immensely grateful to everyone below:

All of our Kickstarter supporters who got us started making the film, which led to this book!

The HarperCollins team for believing in this project and helping turn our ideas into reality—specifically Annette Bourland, Barbara Herndon, Andrea Vinley Converse, Jacque Alberta, Sara Merritt, Londa Alderink, and Ron Huizinga.

Our film producers: Penny Edmiston and Jane Kelly Kosek

All the talented cinematographers and photographers: Mike Prickett, Larry Haynes, Noah Alani, Layne Stratton, Mike Nulty, Matt Shuster, Tim McKenna, Mick Curley, Agustin Munoz, and Layne Stratton

Our wonderful friends: Shane and Sofia Beschen, Tom and Cheri Hamilton, Noah and Timmy Hamilton, Jeff Hall, Liza Richardson, Matt and Ian Calderon, and Emily Miller

The editorial team: Carol Martori, Dan Mayfield, and Rommel Mendoza

RED Digital Cinema and G-Technology for their support: James Lucarelli, Jarred Land, Micheal Keegan, and My Phung

Water safety: Dk Walsh, Shaun Walsh, and Raimana Van-Bastolaer

Film sponsors: Neil Ridgeway, Brooke Farris, Dylan Slater, Stephen Bruner, and Kimberly Devitt

Travel support: Kristin and Quinn Campbell, Caliche, Dara Ahmed and Ian Lyon, Neil Lumsden and Brian Rose, Francis Chute Hasbun, Mike and Toby Neal, Mark Winson, Matt Laskey, and Jon Roseman